To _____

From _____

THE REAL VOYAGE OF DISCOVERY CONSISTS NOT IN SEEKING NEW LANDSCAPES BUT IN HAVING NEW EYES.

MARCEL PROUST

Don't Look Back

Illustrated by
Mary Engelbreit

Andrews and McMeel
A Universal Press Syndicate Company
Kansas City

10 9 8 7 6

ISBN: 0-8362-4626-8

Written by Jan Miller Girando

Don't Look Back

As you travel through life
there are always those times
when decisions just have to be made…

…when the choices are hard,
and solutions seem scarce…

...and the rain seems
to soak your parade!

There are some situations
where all you can do
is to simply let go and move on…

…gather courage together
and choose a direction
that carries you toward a new dawn.

So pack up your troubles
and take a step forward—
the process of change can be tough...

THERE IS ALWAYS ONE MOMENT
IN CHILDHOOD WHEN THE DOOR
OPENS AND LETS THE FUTURE IN.

— GRAHAM GREENE

...but think about all
the excitement ahead
if you can be stalwart enough!

There could be adventures
you never imagined
just waiting around the next bend…

HAVE · A · GOOD · TRIP

...and wishes and dreams
just about to come true
in ways you can't yet comprehend!

Perhaps you'll find friendships
that spring from new interests
as you challenge your status quo…

…and learn there are so many
options in life,
and so many ways you can grow!

Perhaps you'll go places
you never expected
and see things that you've never seen…

…or travel to fabulous,
faraway worlds
and wonderful spots in between!

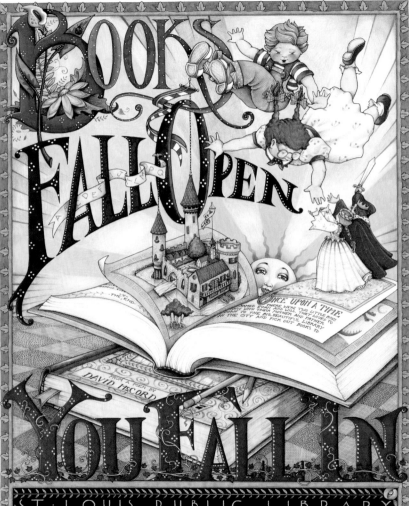

BOOKS FALL OPEN

YOU FALL IN

FROM A POEM BY DAVID McCORD

ONCE UPON A TIME

ST. LOUIS PUBLIC LIBRARY

Perhaps you'll find warmth
and affection and caring—
a "somebody special" who's there…

...to help you stay centered
and listen with interest
to stories and feelings you share.

Perhaps you'll find comfort
in knowing your friends are
supportive of all that you do…

BE MINE

…and believe that whatever
decisions you make,
they'll be the right choices for you!

So keep putting one foot
in front of the other...

WE MUST LAUGH & WE MUST SING, WE ARE BLEST BY EVERYTHING, EVERYTHING WE LOOK UPON IS BLEST

…and taking your life
day by day.

There's a brighter tomorrow
that's just down the road.

Don't look back—
you're not going that way!

Always take the Scenic Route

HAVE·A·WONDERFUL·LIFE